It's Back to School We Go!

It's Back to School We Go!

First Day Stories From Around the World

Ellen Jackson

Illustrated by Jan Davey Ellis

THE MILLBROOK PRESS
Brookfield, Connecticut

To Kathy Jackson and Deb Jackson.
—EJ

For Maureen Reedy, a wonderful teacher.
—JDE

Text copyright © 2003 by Ellen Jackson
Illustrations copyright © 2003 by Jan Davey Ellis
All rights reserved

Published by The Millbrook Press, Inc.
2 Old New Milford Road
Brookfield, Connecticut 06804
www.millbrookpress.com

Library of Congress Cataloging-in-Publication Data
Jackson, Ellen B., 1943-
It's back to school we go : first day stories from around the world / Ellen Jackson ;
illustrated by Jan Davey Ellis.
p. cm.
Summary: In easy-to-read text, describes what the first day of school might be like for a child
in Kenya, Kazakhstan, Canada, Australia, Japan, China, Peru, Germany, India, Russia, and the
United States. Includes bibliographical references.
ISBN 0-7613-2562-X (lib. bdg.) — ISBN 0-7613-1948-4 (trade)
1. Education—Juvenile literature. 2. First day of school—Juvenile literature. [1. Education.
2. First day of school.] I. Ellis, Jan Davey, ill. II. Title.
LB1556.J33 2003   371'.002—dc21   2002152485

Printed in Hong Kong
lib: 5 4 3 2 1
tr.   5 4 3 2 1

Author's Note

Each of the eleven children portrayed in this book is a composite of several real individuals. Obviously, every country provides a variety of educational opportunities and no one child can represent them all. Some children live in villages; others in cities. Some schools have computers and science labs; others don't even have desks or books.

But children everywhere go to school. Children everywhere want to learn about the world and their place in it. In this book, I have tried to capture the diversity of school experiences, to compare and contrast the lives of children from different cultures, and—most of all—to emphasize their common humanity.

E. J.

CANADA

NORTH AMERICA

UNITED STATES

PERU

SOUTH AMERICA

Achieng

An Eight-Year-Old Girl from Kenya

Jambo! Hello. I, Achieng, am a Luo girl from Kenya. My parents gave me a name that means "sun" because I was born at midday.

Today I walked to school and met my teacher and classmates for the first time. Everyone was busy with chores. The girls swept the floor, while the boys cut the grass with pangas, or machetes. Afterward, we sat on a straw mat and began our lessons. I will learn health, arithmetic, and to read and write in Kiswahili.

At noon it began to rain. The noise of drops hitting the tin roof was so loud that we began to giggle. The teacher stopped talking. When the storm was over, we went outside, and I ate mandazi, or fried bread, for lunch.

I love sports, so I played soccer with some of the other children after school. We used two termite nests for goalposts.

When I got home, I helped my mother tend the shamba, or garden. We are growing cassava, potatoes, and beans. Tonight we will eat red bean stew for dinner. Then Grandmother will tell us stories about lion, hyena, and the other African animals.

Children in Kenya

★ Some Kenyans live in huts on small plots of land, where they grow corn, potatoes, cassava, pineapples, and mangoes. Others live in modern cities.

★ Children go to school six days a week from January to November. The students help keep the school clean. In the classroom, they sit on a straw mat or share a desk. Books and paper are scarce.

★ Kenyans love to play soccer. They sometimes use a bundle of rags for a ball and a termite nest for a goalpost. They also enjoy basketball, volleyball, and a board game called *mancala* that is played with seeds or shells.

★ Elephants, leopards, cheetahs, monkeys, lions, and zebras make their home in Kenya. Kenyans enjoy telling stories about these animals.

Anton

A Seven-Year-Old Boy from Kazakhstan

Salam Aleikum! I send you greetings from Almaty, Kazakhstan, where I live with my mother, father, sister Marina, and Grom the dog. Today, September 1, was my first day of school. How excited I was!

After a breakfast of yogurt, cakes, and tea, I got dressed, putting on my good jacket and my boots. My father presented me with a bag of candles, pencils, and sweets in honor of this important day. At school I will learn to read and write in Kazakh and Russian, the main languages spoken in Kazakhstan. I will also learn to use a computer.

When it was time to go, the whole family walked to my new school, No. 115. On the way, my mother gave me a coin to buy a bouquet of flowers at the bazaar for my new teacher.

After we arrived, the opening celebrations began. The older children performed a dance, and one of the teachers gave a speech. Then a girl rang a bell. She had been chosen to carry a new child around the room for all the students to see. She picked me! Everyone laughed and applauded, and I was very happy.

Children in Kazakhstan

★ In Kazakhstan, the first day of school is a time of celebration. Each child brings flowers for the teacher. One new student is chosen to be carried around the room and introduced to the others.

★ Children play a racing game called *Bayga*. They also play *Jebeshkek Bukender*, or "Sticky Tree-Stump." A few children pretend to be trees. They squat down and try to touch others who run by. Boys enjoy wrestling, and everyone likes table tennis.

★ A meal might include noodle soup, mutton, cabbage, and *plov*, which is made from raisins, prunes, or apples. *Koy-Bas*, a boiled sheep's head, is often served on New Year's Day.

★ Kazakh music is played on a *dombra*, a two-stringed instrument. But many young people also like rock and roll, and alternative music.

Kendi

A Six-Year-Old Inuit Boy from Nunavut, Canada

Asujutilli! My name is Kendi, and I live in the territory of Nunavut, Canada, a land of ice and snow. My mother made me a parka and caribou mitts for the cold weather. But today was sunny—so I wore jeans, a jacket, and a baseball cap.

I went to my classroom and met Mr. Anawak, my new teacher. Then all the students gathered on the tundra for a special outdoor picnic. The teachers built a fire, and we roasted hot dogs, fish, and caribou meat. I like caribou the best— except when it sticks in my teeth. Some of the children picked blueberries and blackberries and shared them with the rest of us.

Later, we played an Inuit blanket game. A group of older children held a blanket and bounced the smaller ones by pulling the blanket tight. Each child tried to bounce the highest. My show-off sister won the game!

I will be in the first grade tomorrow, when classes begin. I will learn Inuktitut and English, storytelling, science, and math. After school, my brother Steven and I will hunt rabbits down by the river.

Children in Nunavut, Canada

★ Inuit mothers make down-filled parkas, caribou mitts, and crocheted hats called *nassaks* to keep their families warm in the winter. In the classroom and in warmer weather children wear T-shirts and jeans.

★ The school year starts in the middle of August and ends in May. Students study English and Inuktitut, their native language; science; math; and computers. Schools invite Inuit elders into the classroom to share their knowledge.

★ Children hunt for duck eggs in the spring and pick berries in the summer. They enjoy skiing, skating, and dogsledding in the winter.

★ Inuit love to hunt and fish. Caribou, seal, arctic char, and *maktaaq*, or raw blubber, are favorite dishes. But Inuit children also watch television and snack on chips, chocolate, and soda.

Jessica

A Nine-Year-Old Girl From Australia

G'day! My name is Jessica, and I live in Sydney, Australia, with my mum and dad. It's the first day of the new term, and I'm in year four. That means I'm old enough to join the debating team and sing in the choir.

After breakfast, I put on my school uniform, including a hat for the sun. Then I walked to school. Our class lined up in the yard. My new teacher, Mr. Elton, had us sit outside and make up some classroom rules. Briana said she thought chewing gum shouldn't be allowed in the classroom—just as I blew a big bubble.

The teacher read us a funny story about cow-dung custard, by a famous Australian writer. Then we worked in the school bushland doing some serious weed busting. I especially love the blue flax lilies and the Mickey Mouse plants that grow here.

I bought a popper at the canteen for snack. In the afternoon we were assigned computer keypals in Germany. I e-mailed my keypal and told her about kookaburras, koalas, and other Australian animals. Some people call Australia "The Lucky Country." I know I'm lucky to live here!

Children in Australia

★ The school term begins at the end of January and ends in mid-December. School hours are from 9:00 to 3:00. Many Australian children wear uniforms, including hats to protect them from the sun's strong rays.

★ Lunch might include a meat pie or a sandwich and a fruit drink in a box, called a *popper*. For dinner Australians like fast foods, steaks, and salads. Some people eat kangaroo-tail soup or smoked crocodile.

★ Children play T-ball, rugby, soccer, and cricket, a game played with a bat and ball.

★ The Australian wilderness, called the *bush* or *bushland,* is home to kookaburras, kangaroos, koalas, duck-billed platypuses, and other unusual animals.

Misaki

A Six-Year-Old Girl from Japan

Konichiwa! I am Misaki from Japan, and today was my first day of school. I was both afraid and excited as I walked to school with my friends Naoki and Reina. I wondered if my classmates would like me and if the homework would be too hard. We first graders will learn Japanese, arithmetic, social studies, sewing, music, and art.

At school, the principal greeted everyone and gave a speech about safety. He reminded us to come early tomorrow to help weed the school yard and scrub the floors.

Before going into my classroom, I took off my shoes and put on a pair of slippers. Everyone bowed to the teacher, Miss Tanaka. She showed us how to make an origami bird by folding paper. Then she let me feed the poisonous snake that lives in a tank in our classroom.

At noon, two children served us rice with seaweed sauce and quail eggs. They had prepared it themselves in the cafeteria. I will have a turn to help with lunch on Friday.

I played dodgeball at recess. Then our class had a tug-of-war with another class. School wasn't scary after all. I think I will like it!

Children in Japan

★ The Japanese school year begins in April. Children attend classes five days a week and two Saturday mornings each month. Once a week children come an hour early to shovel snow, weed the grass, or dust and sweep the floors.

★ Each child carries a *randoseru,* or backpack, that contains pencil cases, notebooks, and other items. Boys usually carry black bags, and girls carry red ones.

★ The children study Japanese characters, or word pictures, called *kanji.* Children learn to write more than one thousand *kanji* while they are in primary school.

★ Japanese children play on jungle gyms and swings. They play tag, soccer, and dodgeball. *Kendo,* or fencing, is another favorite Japanese sport. Children also read, draw, and fold paper to make origami animals.

Jinsong

An Eight-Year-Old Boy From China

Ni-hao! Hello from Shanghai, China. I, Jinsong, am happy to be in the third grade at last. But I slept too long this morning and was almost late. I knotted my red neckerchief quickly while my grandmother put my bowl and chopsticks into my schoolbag. I must do better so I will not shame my family.

At school, the children gathered in the playground to sing the national anthem. The flag was raised. We did some exercises, then marched to our classroom. When the teacher entered, the students stood up together and said, "Hello, teacher."

I am learning Mandarin Chinese, math, geography, English, and calligraphy, or writing. But my favorite subject is brush painting. Wonderful pictures come out of my brush when it touches the paper. Today a large green dragon popped out as if by magic!

After lunch I beat Wu Hao at Ping-Pong. Then we returned to the classroom and studied until 4:30. Twice we rested our eyes to keep from straining them.

Some of my classmates go to the Children's Palace for music and art lessons after school. My family cannot afford to send me, so I will go home and play a video game.

Children in China

★ School starts in September, and children attend six days a week. Some children also enroll in special classes at the Children's Palace, where they learn piano, painting, dancing, science, and sports.

★ Some children go home for lunch. Others bring their own bowls and chopsticks so they can eat at school. Lunch often consists of soup and *manto*, or Chinese bread, and is served by the teacher.

★ Schools award red neckerchiefs for good behavior. Almost everyone has earned one by third grade.

★ Chinese children enjoy sports such as gymnastics, soccer, and Ping-Pong. They play with tops, fly kites, jump rope, watch television, and play video games.

Thomas

A Seven-Year-Old Boy from Peru

Hola! I am Thomas from the Amazon rain forest. I live with my family in a house on stilts beside the river. My father taught me to weave a shigra, or fishnet, from palm fiber and to make jewelry from tagua nuts. He was my first teacher, but now I have another.

This morning my big sister, Katia, and I paddled our canoe to school. My job was to bail water. We must fix that leak! Rose-colored dolphins swam alongside us, and a big snake slithered by. Katia whacked a papaya with her paddle and gave me a piece for breakfast.

When we arrived at school, I met my new teacher. Her name is Isabelle, and she is fourteen. The school is a hut with a dirt floor. We have a few desks, a chalkboard, and a map of Peru—but no books. We will learn counting, reading, and writing.

A boy had brought his pet monkey to school. When the monkey ran outside and climbed a tree, Isabelle made a rule: No pets at school! Then she taught us the national anthem of Peru. Katia and I sang it over and over as we paddled home.

Children of the Amazon, Peru

★ The *Riberenos* of Peru live alongside the Amazon River in huts built on stilts for protection from floods.

★ Children learn how to hunt and fish from their parents. They also learn how to grow bananas, rice, and manioc, a plant that can be mashed into flour.

★ The river is like a highway, and even children have their own canoes. Children like to race their canoes, sing, and play tag and hopscotch. Canoes transport many children to school.

★ School is often held in a one-room hut with a dirt floor. Teenagers teach the younger children counting, reading, writing, and geography.

★ Toucans, tanagers, and puffbirds flit through the rain forest. Some *Riberenos* keep monkeys, parrots, or capybaras (large rodents) for pets.

Gunther

A Six-Year-Old Boy From Germany

Guten Tag! Good day. My name is Gunther, and I live in Berlin, Germany. Yesterday my parents took me shopping for a schultute, a large paper cone filled with candy, pencils, candles, crayons, and toys. I decorated it with stickers of lions and tigers, and Father took my picture standing next to it. Father says the schultute will sweeten my first day of school.

Today I went to school on the tram with my parents and Aunt Mutti. Another boy on the tram carried a schultute, but mine was bigger!

First we went to assembly, where the older children sang a song for us. Then the new children and their relatives went to class. My teacher, Mrs. Bader, showed us a letter that some first graders had written to a mouse in America. One day the mouse wrote back! Mice cannot write, so perhaps it was all make-believe. We, too, will learn to write, read, and study maths, science, religion, geography, and local history.

Tonight my family will celebrate my first day, with balloons, pastries, cheese, and lemonade. I will get to eat the candy in my schultute *because* I was good and obeyed the teacher.

Children in Germany

★ The school year begins in late August or early September and ends in July. Children have several short holidays instead of one long one.

★ Class begins at 7:30 or 8:00 and is over at noon. Children study reading, writing, geography, religion (or good behavior), science, and mathematics, or *maths*.

★ Before beginning school, children shop with their parents for a *schultute*, a large paper cone filled with school supplies, presents, and candy. The cones vary in size from a few inches to a few feet tall.

★ Children have their photographs taken with the *schultuten* and bring them to school. Most schools celebrate the first day with a party for the new students and their relatives.

23

Rajani

An Eight-Year-Old Girl from India

Namaste! In Hindi that means hello! I am Rajani from a village near Bangalore, India. It is July, and our school holiday is over. I am excited to be starting grade three!

Today I took the bus to school and found my new classroom. Our class sang a hymn in Sanskrit. We prayed that the school year would be happy for both teachers and students. Our first lesson was geography, followed by English, Hindi, and science.

In the afternoon we had maths, my favorite subject. I hope to become an accountant if my parents allow me to stay in school. My uncle says that boys need school more than girls. I think he is wrong. But Indian children must respect their elders, so I do not argue.

After school, I cared for the baby while my mother made dal and chapati. Then I fed Kapila the cow, whom we keep for milk and butter. I have heard that American children eat cows. I don't know how they could do such a thing!

The electricity was on, so my parents watched a Hindi movie on television. I tried to do my homework, but I was tired and soon fell asleep.

Children in India

★ The school term begins in July and ends in March or April. Children go to school six days a week, including Saturday. Some families believe school is more important for boys than for girls.

★ In school, children study Hindi, English, and Sanskrit, a language used in Hindu religious books. Boys and girls sit on separate sides of the room.

★ Indians eat many different kinds of food, including *dal,* or lentil stew, and *chapati,* a flat bread. They also enjoy pizza. People who practice the Hindu religion consider cows sacred and do not eat beef.

★ Indian children like movies and Hindi pop music. Everyone enjoys cricket and *kho-kho,* a chasing game played by men, women, and children.

Nadia

A Seven-Year-Old Girl from Russia

Privyet! *Greetings from Moscow, Russia. Today was the first day of school—a time of fun and excitement in my country. For breakfast I ate a bowl of buckwheat porridge. Then I put on my white pinafore. Mama tied a ribbon in my hair and gave me a bouquet of flowers for my new teacher. I was proud!*

A band played music as the children, including my brother, Viktor, and I, gathered at the school gate under a banner. Our teachers welcomed us and showed us our classrooms. Then school was over, and the fun began.

Our family took the metro to a park. We saw the Russian space shuttle and rode on the Ferris wheel. We ate blinis, and I watched a show with puppets that looked like huge dolls. Everything was free in honor of the Day of Knowledge.

When we got home, Papa and Viktor played chess. Mama made borscht, and I listened to a CD.

Tomorrow at school, the hard work will begin. Viktor talks of piles of homework taller than a mountain. Papa says he is teasing—that I will learn to read and write. But first I must learn the alphabet.

Children in Russia

★ The school year begins on September 1 and ends in May. On the first day of school, called the Day of Knowledge, children bring flowers to their teachers and enjoy special events and entertainment.

★ Students study nature, mathematics, Russian, English, and local history in elementary school. Children attend classes six days a week and have several hours of homework each night.

★ Many Russian foods, such as *borscht,* or beet soup, and *blinis,* thin pancakes filled with salmon or meat, are famous throughout the world. Russian children like to play chess and listen to CDs.

★ Russians use the Cyrillic alphabet. It has thirty-three letters and is very different from the English alphabet.

Casey

A Nine-Year-Old Boy from California

Hi there! *Casey's my name. The alarm clock rang way too early this morning. I had a waffle and orange juice for breakfast. Then I grabbed my backpack and lunch, and rode to school on my bike, thinking, "Fourth grade, here I come!"*

At school, I sat near my friend Kevin. Mrs. Workman, our teacher, asked us to say something about ourselves. When my turn came, I said, "I have a cat named Midnight, and my favorite sports are skateboarding and baseball."

Mrs. Workman read a story about John Glenn. She said we will learn division in math this year. We'll also study reading, writing, space, weather, and the history of California. I like the first day of school because the teachers do most of the talking and we don't have much homework.

At lunch, I traded my cookie for Kevin's chips, and then we played kickball. After school, I signed up for Little League. Mom is making hamburgers for dinner and pumpkin pie for dessert. It's my turn to wash the dishes. Last night my brother and I got into a soapsuds fight. Dad says we better not try that again!

Children in the United States

★ Nine out of ten children go to public school, which is free. The school year usually starts in September, and children attend classes five days a week.

★ Children in the primary grades study reading, writing, social studies, math, computers, art, and science. Some children play in the school band or sing in the choir.

★ Baseball is a popular sport, and some children play on Little League (baseball) teams. Children also enjoy skateboarding, soccer, hockey, kickball, arts and crafts, and reading.

★ Children in the United States eat many different foods, including cereal, juice, sandwiches, hamburgers, hot dogs, pizza, fish, pie, cookies, and ice cream.

Bibliography

Ayer, Elinor. *Germany: In the Heartland of Europe.* New York: Benchmark Books, 1996.

Bonvillain, Nancy. *The Inuit.* New York: Chelsea House Publishers, 1995.

Bradley, Catherine. *Kazakhstan.* Brookfield, Connecticut: The Millbrook Press, 1992.

Cheng, Pang Guek. *Kazakhstan.* New York: Marshall Cavendish, 2001.

Corona, Laurel. *Kenya.* San Diego, California: Lucent Books, Inc., 2000.

Dolan, Sean. *Germany.* Philadelphia: Chelsea House Publishers, 1999.

Dramer, Kim. *People's Republic of China.* New York: Children's Press, 1999.

Geography Department. *Kazakhstan.* Minneapolis, Minnesota: Lerner Publications Company, 1993.

Hancock, Lyn. *Nunavut.* Minneapolis, Minnesota: Lerner Publications Company, 1995.

Heinrichs, Ann. *China.* New York: Children's Press, 1997.

Heinrichs, Ann. *Japan.* New York: Children's Press, 1998.

Kelly, Andrew. *Australia.* New York: The Bookwright Press, 1991.

Kindersley, Barnabas and Anabel. *Children Just Like Me.* New York: Dorling Kindersley Publishing, Inc., 1995.

Kurian, George Thomas, ed. *World Education Encyclopedia.* New York: Facts on File Publications, 1988.

Lassieur, Allison. *The Inuit.* Mankato, Minnesota: Bridgestone Books, 2000.

Lord, Richard. *Germany.* Edited by Ellen White. Milwaukee, Wisconsin: Gareth Stevens Publishing, 1999.

McNair, Sylvia. *India.* Chicago: Children's Press, 1990.

Menzel, Peter. *Material World: A Global Family Portrait.* San Francisco, California: Sierra Club Books, 1994.

Miyazima, Yasuhiko. *China.* Milwaukee, Wisconsin: Gareth Stevens Publishing, 1988.

Morrison, Marion. *Peru.* New York: Children's Press, 2000.

Murrell, Kathleen. *Russia.* New York: Alfred A. Knopf, 1998.

Pateman, Robert. *Kenya.* New York: Marshall Cavendish, 1994.

Pitkanen, Matti A. *The Children of China.* Minneapolis, Minnesota: Carolrhoda Books, Inc., 1990.

Rajendra, Vijeya. *Australia.* New York: Marshall Cavendish, 1994.

Shelley, Rex. *Japan.* New York: Marshall Cavendish, 1990.

Srinivasan, Radhika. *India.* New York: Marshall Cavendish, 1990.

Sumio, Uchiyama. *India.* Milwaukee, Wisconsin: Gareth Stevens Publishing, 1988.

Torchinskii, Oleg. *Russia.* New York: Marshall Cavendish, 1994.

Winslow, Zachary. *Kenya.* Philadelphia: Chelsea House Publishers, 2000.

Yanagi, Akinobu. *Australia.* Milwaukee, Wisconsin: Gareth Stevens Publishing, 1988.

Web Resources

National Geographic Kids Home Page
http://www.nationalgeographic.com/kids/
Games, postcards, animals, maps

ePALS.com
http://www.epals.com/
The largest on-line classroom community.
Provides student-safe e-mail with children all
over the world.

Say Hello to the World
http://www.ipl.org/youth/hello
How to say "hello" in thirty different
languages.

Really Cookin'
http://www2.whirlpool.com/html/homelife/
cookin/morekrec.htm
Kids' recipes from around the world.

Farm Animals Around the World
http://www.enchantedlearning.com/coloring
/farm.shtml
Facts and coloring pages featuring farm
animals around the world.

Children's Games from Around the World
http://www.rice.edu/projects/topics/edition
11/games-section.htm
Tag, tops, jump rope, ball games, and many
other games from around the world. Stories
and instructions on how to play.

About the Author

Ellen Jackson has written more than fifty fiction and nonfiction books for children. Her best-selling Cinder Edna has won many awards, as has Looking for Life in the Universe and Turn of the Century. The last, also illustrated by Jan Davey Ellis, received a starred review in Booklist, a pointered review from Kirkus, and was an American Bookseller "Pick of the Lists."

Her most recent Millbrook title is My Tour of Europe by Teddy Roosevelt, Age 10, illustrated by Catherine Brighton, an edited version of an actual childhood diary by the former U.S. president.

A former elementary school teacher who now writes full-time, Ellen Jackson lives in Santa Barbara, California, where she enjoys exploring tide pools along the shore.

About the Illustrator

Jan Davey Ellis earned her bachelor of fine arts degree in painting, after which she painted all sorts of things, from jewelry to wall murals. She has been illustrating children's books for the past ten years, and has shared credits with Ellen Jackson on many titles, including a wonderfully reviewed series of four books on the seasons: Winter Solstice, Summer Solstice, Autumn Equinox, and Spring Equinox. Other books she has illustrated recently include Hasty Pudding, Johnnycakes, and Other Good Stuff by Loretta Frances Ichord and A Sampler View of Colonial Life by Mary Cobb.

The artist lives in Ohio with her husband, three daughters, and a cat.